Why do Hot Women Love The Alpha Man?

Pickup Artists Secrets

CONTENTS

- Why be Assertive but never Aggressive
- What are the specific Beta Male Behaviors to Avoid

CHAPTER 1

How to be the Real Alpha Man

Women are attracted to real men – the "Man's Man." This book will show you how to evolve into such a man – the Alpha. It will make you the masculine man you were destined to be but have not evolved into it completely yet. Trust me when I say this – women will love you for it!

In this book, you will learn the following:

- How to attract women by just being yourself?
- How to get "unstuck" and grow up into a Alpha Man?
- How to stop chasing women and turn the tables on her?
- How to take personal control of your destiny?
- How to stop giving away your power to others?
- How to get over your insecurities?

- How to stop needing a woman to need you?

- How to give up the "beta man" behaviour?

- How to grow constantly to get an unfair advantage in attracting women?

Why women like the Real Alpha Man

Alpha is the first letter of the Greek alphabet. In astronomy, it is the brightest star in a constellation. In common parlance, alpha means to be the first.

Alpha males are guys who seem to be leading the pack, the hunter, the ever-reliable male god. They are all around us, in the ranks burly blue collar workers to the impeccable corporate leaders. So why do women like alpha males; or do they?

Women do not only like alpha males; they adore them! Alpha males are the stuff that women's romantic imaginations are of. These are men who get women's

8

attention, wherever they go.

The attraction lies in the power seemingly possessed by alpha males. It's not really just about the money, but it is about strength in character and the ability to be respected by his peers.

A woman defines an alpha male as someone who is vocal about what he wants and who does everything to get it. An alpha male is not just cocky our loud, but there is a semblance of authority in his voice that seems to attract others, male or female. An alpha male is filled with confidence about his appearance, though he may not be handsome and is confident about his intelligence, though he may not be a Wharton graduate.

In the animal kingdom, the alpha males are those who lead the pack with an aggressive behavior. The animals have their own social structure where the alpha or the dominant males get to mate with the females, with the principle that the alpha males will most probably produce better offsprings. Same goes for the alpha males in the society of humans.

Women describe alpha males as those with an innate superiority and who literally leads the pack. These are males who are aggressive and assertive despite their limitations.

To be able to understand an alpha male, one has to get to know his characteristics:

How to show her that you are a Born Leader

Alpha males are born to lead the pack. They are known to be the peacemakers and the ones responsible for stopping fights after and aggression usually started off by a bully. These men are usually dignified men who have leadership capabilities, and they sometimes rule their world. An alpha male is a no nonsense leader who cannot be dictated upon and who stands by his principles.

Gandhi is an alpha male. He was a charismatic leader who refused to be pressured into giving up his cause. He was able to win his battle by espousing non-violence.

Microsoft's czar Bill Gates is an example of an alpha male who continues to change the world and its people. There are many alpha males in a variety of settings, all of whom have provided inspiration and great leadership to their sectors. Most alpha males are attracted and married to strong and outstanding women.

How to show your Confidence

Alpha males are so sure of themselves but not to point of being cocky. They have high self esteem, believing that they have the power to do anything they want and to achieve their dreams. They know they have that special something within them, but they do not boast nor talk about their strength.

Women are attracted to the alpha because of the confidence that emanates from them. This confidence manifests itself in the way he carries himself and the way he deals with others. This confidence is shown in the way he does things and treats other people.

The alpha male's high self esteem makes him confident that he can get the best girl in town. The truth is, the girls usually flock around him.

How to be Assertive

Being confident of himself and in what he can achieve, the alpha male is always assertive but not to the point of being pushy. He knows what he wants and how to get it. He asserts his rights and the rights of his friends. This may be the reason why alpha males are so popular with the pack. He leads them and gives them protection.

Women love the alpha male for being assertive, of being able to know he can do it and doing something to achieve what he wants to do.

Born leaders, confident and assertive. These are the qualities that make women swoon over the alpha male. Need we say more?

Why being in her 'Friend Zone' can lead to problems

Let me begin by narrating a true incident about myself. I was about 33 years only when I was once driving down a highway and pulled up at a roadside leisure-spot. My eyes chanced to come across a group of girls hanging out at a café off the road. I stopped and one babe happened to make eye contact with me. I stopped and decided to strike a conversation. I wanted the address of a place. The woman came forward and tried to help me. I stopped, ordered for a cup of coffee and also offered the chick. She said no, and moved on.

After the coffee, I decided to move on. I barely moved a kilometer away, when I caught sight of that same babe alone, waiting for transport. I offered to drop her home. She gave a coy smile and then came into my car on the next offer. Soon, I realized I had got her in bed, and it was the next morning. So just striking a conversation of the right kind gave me a one night stand. However, it won't be out of place to mention that I'm still in touch with this hottie till date.

Have you ever tried being friends with a girl, orbiting around her as the months go by, hoping that she will fall for you someday or the other? Lots of guys do this, particularly the shy ones. They listen attentively as their female friends tell them about what jerks the real men in their lives have been. Believe me, I've experienced this.

The low point came when a female friend of mine, whom I had a huge crush on, wanted me to come and hang out with her at her apartment. "Great!" I thought. I thought this was the moment I'd been waiting for a long time. However, the truth was quite different from my expectation. We sat in her living room and like a nice guy, I agreed to her prospect, which included spending good two hours meticulously going over everything that her friend across the street (a druggie bartender) said to her at dinner last night. "He laughed and called me silly. Do you think I have a chance?" I did what I could do best — I told her that I thought he was a jerk, and that she could get someone better. I gave her all the genuine, logical reasons why that were true. She told me she agreed with me. (Girls with the "wrong guy" always agree that he's wrong. Then, of course, they forget it and have sex with those "wrong guys", as she did.)

If there's any justice in the world, eventually women will come around to like the nice guys. The truth is, sometimes they do like nice guys, but that is usually when they're older. By that time, they've mostly already had kids by some jerk who escaped on them and the kids and the thought of settling down with a weak-willed man who will stick around and bring in a steady income is starting to have an appeal. Women just simply don't like worthless men for more than friends. And when you act like a nice guy and follow the woman's agenda, and submit to her to make decisions, she doesn't respect you.

Nice guys want the woman to decide where they go to eat and when they have sex. They have no clue that her respect for him automatically drops, and she drops them down into the permanent "just friends" category and then there is no hope left. And that's why the nice guy doesn't get to have sex.

Like I said, women don't like to take the lead in matters relating to sex. You, as the man in the relationship, need to take that responsibility and lead the way. That's what women want you to do, and mark my words; they love it when you do it.

What is meant by the Alpha Man

Alpha males assume leadership and take decisions. By this I mean that they act as if they are a natural leader in their setting. Therefore, they don't care much about what others think. They do their own thing and don't seek approval. However, at the same time, they also offer a benefit to those who follow them, whether it's social status, excitement, or stimulating conversation.

When a woman says something sarcastic, the beta male (the nice guy) gets offended, while the alpha male laughs about it because he knows girls are like his silly little sisters. And when a woman later regrets her sarcasm, and learns it was really no big deal to the alpha male, she gives him big points for that.

Many social interactions that we engage in have sub-currents of dominance and submission. Studies of social situations have shown that dominant people will mark their territory in various nonverbal ways, such as taking up space with their bodies, using a louder voice, controlling conversations, and using strong eye contact. People around the alpha male tend to get sucked into his reality because he's unusual, interesting and makes them feel comfortable. The alpha male doesn't feel possessive or jealous over a woman because he isn't needy, and he thinks out of the box. He also doesn't suppress women by putting them up on a pedestal. Because of this, he knows that any woman would feel lucky to have him, so if any one particular woman doesn't fall for him, then that's her loss, and not his.

Whereas the beta male is nervous, has low social status, is typically a follower rather than a leader, usually feels secretly resentful of successful guys, has low self-esteem, and is clingy, needy and desperate with women.

An honest confession: I used to be a beta male at one time. I was at that time really depressed and resentful. I desperately wanted a babe as I felt that having one would make my life worth living. Once I got a girl and could have as much sex as I wanted, I thought, my life would be wonderful.

It wasn't until later that I learnt that I had this exactly backwards. It wasn't until I prepared myself from within and had a life worth living that I started attracting the awesome women whom I've had over the years and the wonderful woman who I am currently in a relationship with.

In the next chapter I'm going to share with you some of my secrets on how you can follow the behavior and mindset of an alpha male.

Who are the Beta Males

While I was growing up, my mom, aunts, and other older ladies always told me that if I want to get a girlfriend, I would need to be a nice guy. I'd need to constantly buy a girl flowers, give gifts, and take her out for dinner. I thought I'll need to earn a lot of cash in order to give my babe the best of everything. And unfortunately, I took their advice seriously.

Throughout my school and college life, I tried really hard to be the nice guy, the one, girls supposedly preferred. Girls would always say how much they liked what I did, but what I got at the max was a kiss on the cheek. Then in college and thereafter, the advice changed. All of a sudden, it was common knowledge that to be successful with women, you had to act like an asshole rather than a gentleman. I tried the advice out and found that when I acted like a jerk, women responded to me more. However, I still didn't get the results that I wanted. Though I did get laid, it was with a low self-esteem head case. I still had problems with girls preferring other guys to me. I would feel very down in the dumps most of the time.

So I observed the guys, who were successful with women, the ones who weren't, and the ones in between, and I figured out that there are really three types of men. And there's definitely a picking order as far as the women are concerned. At the bottom of the list are the so called nice guys, who make up the majority of the male population.

The nice guy is a man who basically begs for sex. He is someone who approaches a woman with flowers, drives her to a fancy restaurant and buys her expensive dinner with fine wine. Then, after he escorts her to her home, he gets a shock because she doesn't even invite him in. And the worst part is, he doesn't learn anything from this — he's back to the square one. He uses the same techniques on the very next woman.

Once again, I'm not saying that presenting flowers and gifts to your lady love is wrong. What I'm trying to educate about is the fact that you should not do these things with an ulterior motive behind. Just leave things up to the conscience of the woman, and you'll witness miracles.

What's really ironic and bad here is, believe it or not, women consider nice guys to be manipulative. Women think that the nice guy buys her so many things because he wants something in return. "They're only after one thing!" is a common idea that women have about nice guys. However, she feels that he might have the potential to make a dependable relationship, so she may keep him in hand and eventually share the bed with him.

And whether she makes him wait a long time or not will depend on the woman? Some women set four dates as the minimum before she goes to bed with the nice guy, which is like winning the jackpot for him, as many other women make nice guys wait for months before they "get lucky."

And when sex does come, it's a huge event and the

woman makes a big issue about it. He will have to accept her terms and conditions, like when she happens to be in the mood, and act accordingly. And why do you think nice guys don't succeed? The problem with the nice guy is that not only do women consider him to be manipulative; but also they find him boring.

The nice guy talks about practical things like the stock market or how a car engine operates. Sometimes he brags about himself and how much money he makes, implying that he can buy the woman expensive gifts. "How lame," she thinks. Engaging in practical conversation and trying to impress a woman with your smartness and salary is a mistake that 99% of the guys make. It destroys a woman's attraction for you because it communicates neediness and low self-esteem.

If you weren't seeking her approval, you wouldn't have been trying to impress her. Instead if you were a man of high value (an Alpha Male), then she would be the one asking for your approval.

The other problem is that women who are engaged in the mating ritual with a guy absolutely hate logical conversation. It makes her come out of her trance. So refrain from talking about that article on Chinese trade policies you read in The Economist until you're hanging out with your male friends. Don't misunderstand me, but you should not pretend to be an 'arse' around women. In fact, women find it attractive when a guy is skillful in something.

What you should rather do, however, is make sure to speak about interesting topics within your genre of expertise, not mind-numbing things. In fact, something you should begin immediately, if you haven't done this as yet, is to become an expert in something. It doesn't matter what...cooking, art, rock music, South Park trivia, religion, history, and so on.

A man who's an expert is automatically an alpha male in that genre. Just make sure to win her over with the knowledge you both share. And please don't bore her. (When sharing facts, ask yourself, "Would this information be on 'Ripley's Believe It Or Not' or would it be something a dull college professor would say?) All that girls just want to have is fun, as the song goes, and the nice, boring guy isn't fun.

Go to places where singles congregate, and you can perform an interesting 'people watching' exercise by checking out the couples that you see. If the girl looks bored or is constantly chatting on her cell phone, then she's with her boyfriend. If, on the other hand, she's laughing and looks like she's having a great time, then what you're seeing is most likely a pick-up attempt by an alpha male. Moreover, notice that the alpha male picking up a woman has an easy rapport with her. The two of them talk as if they've known each other for years.

The problem with being the nice guy is the mindset that it springs from. A man pleading to a woman is doing it out of insecurity and desperation for her approval and sexual attention.

Want to share the bed with hot chicks? Then keep this first and foremost in mind: The quickest and easiest way to kill any attraction a woman may be starting to feel for you is to feel insecure about yourself, or plead, or to be needy, or to seek approval. When you have the mindset of being desperate to impress, you end up coming across as too strong, too early. You become clingy. It's like you're begging. There's an old saying about banks: they only want to loan you money when you're loaded already. If you genuinely need the money, then you can forget it.

How to avoid being the Beta Male

In addition to being too indecisive, nice guys also tend to be passively aggressive. Women are often being passive-aggressive themselves, thus they are turned off when that particular trait is seen in a man.

What's passive-aggressive? It's being passive until you've been pushed too far, and then turning aggressive all of a sudden. Ever had a woman who expected you to read her mind and then got mad when you couldn't read or read it wrong? That's passive aggressive. Rather, strike the middle ground between passive and aggressive, which is assertive.

What the nice guy does is, he constantly gives in and does whatever the woman wants. Women find this unattractive and eventually they leave him for someone better. The nice guy then has nothing to do other than complain about how he "did everything for her". And there lies the problem...

Nice guys also have issues with jealousy, which is an outcome of their insecurity. Never give off negative vibes to women, telling them that you are suffering from a sense of insecurity. They will keep you as far as possible. When they are looking for guys who will render security to them, how can you show your insecure condition?

Beta males are too dependent; all the happiness they experience comes from the woman. They hate it when she talks to other guys for fear that she'll run away, and he'll lose his source of happiness. The problem with the feelings of jealousy and insecurity that so many beta males have about their women is that it comes from 'the need'. So whenever you feel that way with a girl, soak it up and let go.

When a girl detects a guy is jealous, it's just like saying to her, "Hey, I feel inferior to those other guys you talk to." And having that lack of confidence in yourself makes the girl not feel so confident in you, either. She begins to wonder whether the grass on the other side of the pasture is greener or not. I know it's tough to control your jealousy, but look at it this way: if you knew that you were the man in control, and that you can attract hot chicks and get laid easily, would you care whether your girl is going off and mixing with some other guys? Of course not, because that would be a loss on her part (and you could just get laid by some other chick)!

Okay, so here's a new attitude, I want you to adopt: "I am developing into a high value alpha male." Keep repeating that to yourself throughout the day as an affirmation. By doing this you will at least be able to control your jealousy if not overcome it.

By the way, you may still be wondering what you should actually do if your girl is talking to other dudes. Well, the absolute and worst thing you can do (ironically) is to try to interfere to stop her from doing it. That tells her that she has the higher value, and not you. Instead, the best way to stop such behavior is to say, "Have a good time!" with a tone of complete unfamiliarity when she says she's going to go out to spend time with some other guy. Let her see that it doesn't bother you one bit. Meanwhile, you go and talk with other girls. One good or bad turn deserves another, eh? That turns the tables so that now she's the one worrying about whether you'll leave her for someone else. That sets you up as having the higher value.

Another way to avoid becoming upset at a woman's behavior is not to take the individual woman too seriously or give much attention to what she is thinking. Being overly conscious about a woman's thoughts and feelings is a waste of time, because the bottom line is you can't control what a woman thinks or feels.

Of all God's creation, the woman is definitely the strangest. We all know how difficult it is to understand her, how whimsical she really is and how she reacts most of the time. When you think you've just managed to convince her, she changes and turns against everything that was pre-planned. Poets and song-writers have written about her and some have even praised her for this uncanny habit that makes the woman stand out from the rest of God's creation.

I know every woman is unique but there are more commonalities than differences among them. The next time you're with a woman, try and say "no" to her at some point. Saying "no" can be powerful with women and can do wonders. Nevertheless, do it in a tactful way.

For example:
Her: "Let's go rent a movie."
You: "No, not yet. Let's go in about an hour."

By saying no, you establish your authority and set yourself up as a challenge for the woman. If she views you as a challenge, then she will be enthusiastic in impressing you instead of being bored. If you say YES to everything your woman suggests, then she will soon be saying NO to you, and the worst situation will be in the bedroom. What you need to know is that women resent any sort of crave.

What attracts women about alpha male is that his happiness comes from within, and so he doesn't put the responsibility of his emotional state on her. To be loved by someone, you need to love yourself first. You have to have a passion for your life, and you've got to do what you want. Nice guys have too much of insecurity, and they look down upon themselves more than anyone else. That's why when it comes to matters of love; nice guys really do finish last.

Why you need not be a be a Jerk

On a middle level, just above the nice guy, is the asshole, or jerk. Women prefer assholes to nice guys because assholes aren't boring. Though an asshole creates an emotional roller coaster of drama with his girlfriend, but at least the girl gets the emotional high points along with those low points. In other words, he may make her sob, but he also makes her laugh. And the uncertainty of what's it going to be does create some excitement in her life.

Here's what you need to know about women: in order to be sexually turned on, women need to tune into their emotions instead of their logic. The nice guy makes a grave mistake of appealing to her logic, whereas the jerk appeals to a woman's emotions. Jerks get laid because they get women turned on by being so persistent and then going for the lay. They are sexually aggressive, unlike the nice guys who are sexually passive. While the jerk creates negative emotions within women, at least he makes an effort to create emotions, whereas the nice guy only bores women.

However, it's not all good for the jerks. The types of women who go for jerks are mainly head-cases who have low self-esteem, depression and other emotional issues. Such women often act weird and insecure when it comes to relationships, so they're really not the kind of women a well-adjusted man would want to go for in any case. Jerks do get laid, but that doesn't mean you have to be a jerk.

What is good news is that there is this higher level of men, whom I call the alpha males throughout this book, who bring about positive emotions within women with no real negatives as such.

How much Self Respect do you have

Before I proceed further, I want to share another observation with you. Have you ever noticed that too often, men are willing to go against what they think, feel, and believe because there is a woman available to them? And the thing is, the men KNOW that what they're doing is going to turn out badly, but they do it anyhow because they want to be with a girl in some way.

By the same token, many men are willing to let the women they're with walk all over them and treat them like crap because they're getting sex out of the deal (if they're lucky, anyway). Us boys have a name for this behavior. It's called being "whipped."

We've all had a friend at one time or another who's suffered from this condition. He's a cool guy, a good friend, but suddenly he meets a woman, and he can't go out drinking because he's got to pick her car up from the shop or take her kid out to the park, or whatever task, she has assigned him. And it's not the fact that she needs him to do things for her, it's the fact that he gives up any sense of what his life was in order to please her.

The problem that comes from this situation is that the guy often not only loses the respect of his friends, but also the respect of the woman he's with. The very person he's trying hardest to please begins to resent him and take him for granted. This is why having rules and standards is important?

It comes down to a matter of SELF-RESPECT.

People who have no code, no rules by which they live their lives, no standards by which they hold themselves up to, are weak people. They look for others to give them an identity, to give them a purpose.

However, having rules and standards allows you to define who you are and stand on your own two feet. People who know what they are, and are willing to do in life, garner respect from others.

Most unhealthy relationships stem from the problem of weakness in one of the partners. Typically, women want a dominant man in a relationship. And when I say dominant, I DON'T mean the ball-gag, chains, and leather whips kind-of dominant. I mean a guy who takes control of the relationship and is a source of strength for the woman he's with. A man who makes her feel safe and eliminates uncertainty from her life.

But the woman aside, it's more about making YOU happy. It's about having respect for yourself, and what you want out of life. If you have in mind a certain type of woman you want to be with, don't lower your standards just to get laid or whatever. That's not respecting yourself. Go after the type of woman you want instead of settling for what you can easily get. You'll be happier that way.

If you have a rule, stick to it in the face of provocation. There's a reason you made it a rule in the first place, right? In the end, having rules and standards makes you a more attractive person, because it conveys confidence and conviction, two traits women always find attractive in a man. And as you know, women are complicated beings, and it seems most men are clueless when it comes to dealing with them!

Some guys just aren't ready to learn these rules of attraction. They just simply aren't ready for them yet. If you're afraid of hard work, are lazy, or don't want to change how your life is currently like, then obviously you are wasting your time reading this book.

However, if you're committed to changing what doesn't work, if you really, truly want to have that feeling of a supremely confident ladies man and carry that with you wherever you go, then you definitely need to continue reading. In this book, you will discover everything you need to change your life for the better!

Good luck, my friend.

CHAPTER 2

How to Show the Alpha Attitude

Alpha vs Beta body language

Watch a man with high status--Brad Pitt, George Clooney, or the CEO where you work--and you'll notice that they move differently than the rest of us. They give off vibes that they are the 'hot stuff', and because of that, women get soaking wet over them. You, too, can create that aura that makes you attractive to women.

There are certain personality traits that you need to develop and must do so fast, if you are contemplating the 'success with women'. Your entire outlook must change and so also your attitude and behavior.

Remember, women are very sensitive beings and have inborn skills to read body language.

Have you ever noticed the way your friends look when they 'feel like shit'? They're looking down at the ground with their arms crossed, slouching, and displaying other non-alpha behaviors. This is quite common in beta males. Now, think about the guys. They've got girls all over them and some great body language going on with that.

So here are some body language pointers (and by the way, if you think they're easy, you're right... you can make these changes as early as tonight and have even the hottest girls clamoring for your attention):

- Relax. This is the most important mental state for you to be in. Don't allow yourself to feel worried. Just let your worries go, since you can't solve any problem by worrying. So suck it up, and quit thinking about what might go wrong. Just live life - Now and here in the moment.

I know what I just said is easier said than done (to use an

old — but relevant in this case — cliché). You've spent your whole life up until now dwelling on thoughts that make you feel worried. But what is this emotion we call "worry"? When you think about it, it's simply the fear of what might happen in the future. Essentially you're punishing yourself by feeling upset before anything bad has happened. It's illogical to take imaginary tension. Always give tension to her, never take tension. Stress and tension only give you heartaches and increase toxins in the body, leading to the bigger health issues in life. Get up, move on and don't let the grass grow under your feet. There are plenty of pebbles on the beach. Don't go brooding over one single female. Look for attention from others, and you'll be a happier man for it.

- Avoid nonverbal behaviors that are the opposite of relaxation:

    Raising your shoulders.
    Wrinkling your forehead.

Fidgeting with your hands and/or legs.

Tightening your facial muscles.

- Relax all your muscles and slow down all of your movements a notch. Alpha males generally move unhurriedly, as if they are in control of time itself. Beta males are nervous and make jerky movements. Imagine you are standing and walking through a swimming pool, where your movements are slow and fluid.

- Relax your eyes and eyelids. Beta males hold their eyelids wide open because they are so nervous. Their eyes dart all around. Instead let your eyelids rest. Look straight ahead. Only give things your attention if they interest you. While you're out and about, do the affirmation to yourself, "I am sexual, I am relaxed, and I am in control."

- Feel masculine and powerful. Visualize that you

are the man. The masculine aspect should rule. Do things in your life that make you feel manly, like lifting weights and working out with a 'punching bag'. Take care of your health. Check your physique in front of a mirror time to time. And also remember that you're a man of high value and esteem. Treat your entire self well. You need to respect your body before you want others to do the same. Does all of this sound right to you? You might think, "This is the height of crap!" But try the advice out and then come back again to this book.

- Feel comfortable in your own skin. An alpha male is happy with or without any particular woman, since he views women as sources of fun in his life —no more and no less. Take the mindset that of course women want you, but it's no big deal either way.

- Spread out your body and take up space. Take up space with your arms, legs, and chest. Keep your neck straight with your back so that your head is held high. (Something that helped me get used to keeping my neck straight was removing the pillow from my bed. After all, it's a major challenge to have optimal posture when your neck is bent for 8 hours every night.)

How to be the Hot Guy in every situation

A lot of other seduction methods talk a lot about picking up women in groups (and in fact, some of the nightclub methods are based on working in groups). I don't talk a lot about being in groups in this book, because the bottom line (in my opinion), is that you should only be in a group with a chick's friends AFTER you've slept with her. And at that point, as long as you remained chilled out, you've got nothing to be concerned about. Having said that, however, here a few simple pointers to be an alpha male in a group situation...

- Always be the most relaxed person, no matter what the group situation is. If someone else is affecting your reality, then they have dominance over you.

- Be talkative. It literally does not matter what you're talking about... just keep those gums flapping. DON'T ANALYZE ANYTHING. Save all self-reflection until LATER. Just let your mind flow, and keep talking.

- Let nothing affect your reality. If someone says something to get a raise out of you, don't allow it. Mainly just follow these three things, and you'll ALWAYS remain alpha in a group setting. (You may not always be at the very top of every group, because hey, what if the President is in your group? However, you'll at least be near the top,

45

and that's all that matters.)

Notice something about those three rules? They're all INTERNAL. Just have your internals in order, and you'll do fine in any group situations. There's no need to have any pickup material memorized or to make a big deal about any mechanics of seduction. As you're being talkative in a group, don't just recite memorized comedy material like the advice around the net sometimes tells you to do, because unless you become VERY GOOD at spouting routines, it'll come across at best as you being their entertainment monkey, and at worst as you looking like a weirdo on drugs.

Besides these three rules, the same guidelines apply for groups as for the one-on-one situations that I've talked about earlier. You should feel free to enter other people's space, only talk about the things that actually interest you, don't smile, unless there's something to smile about. As far as eye contact with men in your group (or men in general, by the way), my question is, who cares? It's truly irrelevant what other guys think of you. The only time you should make eye contact with a guy is when you're saying something to him. When the other guy is talking, don't look at him much, instead looking off to the side. (Ever dealt with a CEO? That's exactly what they do when it comes to eye contact.)

Most importantly, when picking up a girl who's with her friends, try to get the girl by herself and away from the group. For a woman to become horny, she needs to feel relaxed and low-energy. The problem with groups is that they're high energy, which is the very opposite of how you want a woman to feel.

CHAPTER 3

How to make her Chase you

Have you ever read any book on how one could handle a relationship with women by being an alpha male? If you haven't, then keep reading this one and feel the difference.

In order to have sex with a girl in the first place, you need to show your dominant frame of mind. In order to have a successful relationship, all you need to do is to keep this dominant frame continuously.

The principal and most important method I've personally found effective is to apply the concept I call punishment and reward. This means that you reward good behavior and punish the so called bad behavior. If your girlfriend does something you like, then reward her with more of your attention and affection. If she does something you dislike, then punish her by withdrawing your attention.

So many guys do the opposite. When their women behave stupidly or arrogantly, for example, by saying something like, "not tonight", they actually REWARD that behavior by cuddling up with them all night. Make sure to draw the line and not put up with something you don't want. Never compromise with nonsense or stuff that you don't usually put up with anyone else. Be the man and reveal it in proper and appropriate ways.

If you're consistent about this approach, her bad behavior will eventually cease. And if she knows you'll be nice to her when she has earned it, she'll act in ways that cause you to reward her. The ultimate key to success with women is being able to draw the line to how much you are willing to put up with. Always be genuinely ready to walk out at any given moment. Not that you will walk out... but that if your girlfriend knows she has to work to keep you, she will (and also, she'll love you more for it).

Avoid any sort of low-status behavior like arguments. Look at arguments as futile. You may ultimately win the argument, but you will lose the girl. And you wouldn't want that to actually happen, especially if you know you were just 'fooling around' but was not really serious about giving her the ditch or something of the sort. And certainly never insult her.

The best way to do this is to visualize it is as if you're the big grown-up man who's protecting her (almost as if you're her father). By the way, it's important for women to feel like you're the big father figure keeping them safe when they're in your arms. In fact, lots of women may even say things like, "I feel so safe and secure when I'm with you".

Doing 'gentlemanly' things for her helps create the impression of you being the strong man. Open doors for her in an alpha fashion. (Have the mindset that you're stronger than she is, not that you're trying to win her affections.) Walk on the outside of the sidewalk, so that you're the one nearest the street. Be the alpha male in your actions.

Respect yourself, and she'll respect you too. There's no need to defend yourself in order to explain yourself to anyone. Your relationship is a great thing, and will remain that way as long as you remain happy in it.

Women love to chase men, so allow her to chase you. The man's responsibility is for the sex, not the relationship. You make sure you get lots of sex (or else leave her for other girls), and in turn let her do the work when it comes to the relationship. So you can relax most of the time and let her work her butt off. Let her be the one to call you to set up get-together Don't feel like you have to call her too frequently. If she chases you, then she will value you more. It's a simple fact of human psychology. It is often said, so much so that it's almost a cliché, that "whoever cares least controls the relationship." It may be a cliché, but that's because there's so much truth to it.

Let the woman think that she cares more about the relationship than you do. Don't always jump to do things for her. With that said, however, make sure that your girlfriend knows you appreciate what she does. That way she'll feel rewarded for her good behavior. Say things like, "Thank you for cooking dinner for me tonight baby. It was so good! You're the best!" Also tell her things such as, "You please me." Not only does hearing "you please me" make her feel good, but it is also a command in a way. Your girlfriend will want to continue to do the things required to please you.

Basically, the ideal scenario to be in is one in which the woman thinks she's putting a lot of investments into the relationship and that investment is paying off nicely. That way, you stay in control of the relationship. So, although it's best to et her do more of the work, you can (and should) do little things for her at times. Give her unexpected small gifts. They should not be expensive, because the woman might then resent the fact that you're trying to "buy" her affections (which means you're no longer a challenge for her). Make sure to put time and thought into the gifts. One strategy for this is to listen for things that she says she likes. If she tells you she likes a particular song, then surprise her with a CD of the band of her selection.

All women need surprises and spontaneity in their romantic life. One of the best ways to kill a relationship is to make it predictable. Pick a random day of the month and buy her flowers. Take surprise trips. Go on surprise dinner outings. You can accelerate the process of your girlfriend falling in love with you by talking about "destiny" with her.

Even though your good relationship is really sustained by you influencing her behavior and retaining your mindset of an alpha male, don't tell her that. Instead let her live out her life-long fantasies through you.

The vast majority of women want to "embrace" their destiny with the man whom they consider their soul mate. So talk freely about how destiny has brought the two of you together! You'll have more success (and be more in control of the relationship), if you remain a challenge for her. Use the words "I adore you" a few months before finally saying "I love you."

Finally, don't devote yourself 100% to any woman. Have other interests in your life that pull you away from her time to time.

CHAPTER 4

How to Understand
What Hot Women Want

How to avoid looking desperate

Understand her with your Brains, not your Loins. Here's a tricky little secret: almost everyone is a little bit shy and self-conscious to some degree. If they're talking to you because they think you're a person of high value (as a woman will think if she's attracted to you and making conversation), they will feel good if they believe they have been successful in earning your attention.

When you successfully infuse in others the feeling that they've earned your attention, you actually force them to be much more meaningful in what they are saying to you. Once you've figured that out, address what they're really communicating. By doing this you demonstrate your high value instantly.

Let's say someone says to you, "What percentage of our genes do you think we share with chimpanzees?" What's the deeper meaning there? Superficially, they're testing your knowledge. But the real meaning here is that they're trying to show off their knowledge and amaze you with a cool fact. Suppose you're a well-read guy and remember seeing something on National Geographic about how humans and chimps have about 98.5% of the same genes, should you say, "98.5%"? No. Alphas don't play other people's games. A much better response would be, "I don't know, we couldn't be all that similar. Is it 50%?" The person will then feel like they have earned your attention when you tell them how interesting it is that it's 98.5%. (If you feel like you need to display your intelligence, you're seeking the other person's approval and that's a sign that you have low status.)

Suppose someone tells you they just went to Panama City Beach. They say that because they feel excited about the trip they've just gone on and they want you to share in that excitement. The worst thing you could do would be to one-up them by saying, "Man, that's nothing. You should see the beaches and waves in Hawaii!" That statement shows you're not inclined to the other person and this makes them feel like they're not all that special. Instead, get them talking about the things they've enjoyed at the Panama City Beach. Say, "Sweetheart! I've always wanted to go there. I'm curious; what was your favorite part of the trip?" And even though alpha males interrupt when they need to, try not to interrupt people when they are talking about something that is interesting to you. And don't worry too much about it when people interrupt you. People interrupt because they are highly involved in the conversation, which is exactly what you want.

When talking, be focused on them rather than yourself. Take account of the points that people are speaking of and then develop your conversations on those points. This conveys your strong sense of inner contentment and makes you more attractive, knowledgeable and likable in their eyes. Genuinely think about what a woman says and be interested. Every girl is unique, and you have a lot to discover about her. So take your time in your conversations and be a good listener.

What Behaviors you should avoid

Avoid the three behaviors listed below, and you'll instantly separate yourself from 95% of the other guys out there. This is an achievement by itself, for when women sense it; they feel better when you are around.

Don't Lower Your Social Status

Lower status men tend to be modest for fear of displeasing others, and because they want to be considered as polite. Alpha males avoid self-effacing modesty except when it's an obvious joke. High self-confidence is attractive to women. If you think of yourself to be high in status, then a woman will also consider you to be high. It's okay to make an obvious joke about putting yourself down once in a while, like in the following examples (said with a playful tone of voice):

- "I'm so weak, I'm not sure if I can lift that heavy thing." – Spoken by a bodybuilder

- "I wear a leather jacket to compensate because my penis is so small. It's not even half an inch!" - Spoken by a man with huge confidence that obviously does not have sexual insecurities. (That's why he's able to joke about penis size.)

- "I'm unemployed and live in my parents' basement!" – Spoken by a well-dressed man who obviously has loads of money.

Don't be a Braggart

"You should see my Ferrari." "I'm about to get a raise up to six figures a year!" The irony of bragging is what it communicates — you're in great need if you crave for approval. Why else would you have to blow your own bloody trumpet? Avoid directly verbalizing your good qualities and let the woman discover them herself. This showcases your confidence in yourself as well as making you a bit more "mysterious" and "interesting" in her eyes. You've got to make her keep guessing stuff concerning you, your habits, likes and dislikes. If she is always in the know about you, she will always be one up on you. Be an endless source of fascinating discoveries for her, not a blowhard, and you will surely crack it.

Don't criticize others

"Ha ha look at that bum in rags!" When you put others down, you reveal your own insecurities. The homeless guy on the pavement is no threat to you, so why act as if he is? And since women are sensitive creatures who feel sorry for the less fortunate, you'll induce in her a feeling of hatred for you and will force her into taking up for whoever you put down. Some men take great pride in running down others. First and foremost it has nothing to do with your relationship and next, it is morally incorrect to say something unkind about others. Why waste words at the expense of your expensive relationship which you are trying to preserve? It simply reveals a deep sense of insecurity-a weakness that you unknowingly will spill out. There are so many topics to discuss about instead of talking stupidly of others. So just be careful!

How to make yourself likable to women

I've already listed non-verbals that show dominance. However, sometimes dominance signals (such as leaning back) can make you more distant. So when required, you may need to balance your dominance with likeability.

(Too much dominance makes you unlikable.) Be conscious of the following silent techniques that magnetically get a girl in your arms.

- Lean forward when you're sitting across from someone who is telling you something. This communicates interest in what they are saying. However, it's crucial to make sure that the woman is highly interested in you before doing this, since leaning back is a way for you to non-verbally play "hard to get." Once she's interested in you, lean forward to give the impression that you're easy to talk to.

- Directly orient your body and face towards her. Note that you should have dominance established before doing this, since you lose dominance by being more direct with your body language. Don't put the cart before the horse, as it were. Use proper posture at all times while talking to her. You

or imitate others will just make you a blinking clown or a cartoon strip straight out of cartoon network. Your facial expressions and body language generally should reveal that you are completely at ease with the person. This is equally applicable when you are with anybody, in fact. You must endeavor to strike a balance between dominance and likability.

How to bring out the best in her

Ever noticed how successful people behave? Observe them keenly and you will find that they are more generous than the average person when it comes to saying, "Thank you." When someone does a favor for you, they do it because they care about you.

By expressing gratitude towards them, you legitimize their favorable projection of you. Don't say things like "You shouldn't have" that indicate you didn't deserve what they did for you. A person gives things to you because they see you as being worthy of the best. If you kill this attitude of theirs, you convey the message that you're unworthy.

So whenever any woman compliments you or does something nice to you, never belittle it or ignore it. Instead, thank her with the full mindset that you deserved such nice treatment and reward her good behavior. By the way, whenever any woman compliments you, view it as her really saying to you, "I like you. I want you to keep pushing our interaction forward to sex." So say "Thank you!" and it'll almost hypnotically guide her into your bedroom sooner than later!

CHAPTER 5

How to shape the Alpha Physique

Step-by-step Guide to Work Out

The workout I'm going to give you focuses on heavy compound exercises that work on many muscles at a time and include some isolation exercises that will hit any muscle that the compound exercises may have missed. Compound exercises should be the foundation of your workout. Far too many guys in the gym — the ones who just work out before spring break and aren't serious about it — do primarily arm curls and bench press and ignore their legs and back. This leads to poor posture, and no matter how big your upper body gets, skinny chicken legs don't look good. Women really do look at men's legs.

Heavy compound exercises release tons of testosterone in

your body. Besides building muscle, having higher levels of natural testosterone is associated with dominance and sexual power — two traits that are deeply appealing to women.

Here are some guidelines on your weekly workouts. Check them out! More importantly; put them to use IF YOU WANT POSITIVE RESULTS!

Day 1 –

- Three sets of squats. Do 20 reps, 15 reps, and then 12 reps.
- Three sets of stiff-legged dead lifts. Do 20 reps, 15 reps, and 12 reps.
- Two sets of calf raises. Do 20 reps, 15 reps, and 12 reps.
- Two sets of arm curls. Do 12 reps and 10 reps.

Day 2 –

- Rest or cardio.

Day 3 –

- Two sets of weighted forward-leaning dips.4 Do 12 reps and 10 reps.
- Two sets of incline dumbbell presses. Do 12 reps and 10 reps.
- Two sets of lateral raises. Do 12 reps and 10 reps.
- Two sets of overhead dumbbell presses. Do 12 reps and 10 reps.
- Two sets of weighted sit-ups. Do 20 reps and 15 reps.

Day 4 –

- Rest or cardio.

Day 5 –

- Three sets of dead lifts. Do 12 reps, 10 reps, and 8 reps.
- Two sets of weighted chin-ups. Do 12 reps and 10 reps.
- Two sets of weighted pull-ups. Do 12 reps and 10 reps.

- Two sets of dumbbell rows. Do 12 reps and 10 reps.
- Two sets of bent-over lateral raises. Do 12 reps and 10 reps.

Do a warm-up set or two before you go into your main sets, using about 50% and then 75% of your working weights. You may warm up by either jogging on your spot or by skipping with a rope. For example, if you squat 200 pounds during your main sets, you'd warm up by doing 100 pounds for 8 reps, then 150 pounds for 4 reps. You should then feel warmed up to go into your work sets. If not, then you should do 2 or 3 more reps closer to your work weight. In the example, you would do 175 pounds for 3 reps. It's important that you go either to failure or to near-failure. When I say do 20, 15, and 12 sets, that means do the maximum weight that you can lift that particular number of reps. Limit your workouts to 50 minutes. Studies have shown that after that point, your muscles are catabolizing (breaking down) too fast. Give yourself two or three minutes between sets to recover, but remember that you want to be able to do all your exercises within the 50-minute time. Immediately after your workout, consume a mixture of protein and carbohydrates. This puts a stop to the catabolic breakdown that you've started by lifting weights and shifts your body towards anabolism (muscle building). The workout I've outlined is tailored toward muscle growth. If you want to emphasize power, do half the reps. On Tuesday, Thursday, and Saturday, you should do cardiovascular exercises if you need to lose body fat. I recommend doing high intensity interval training. High intensity interval training (HIIT) is short but intense, and studies have shown it to be more effective than moderate intensity training. Moderate training consists of activities such as jogging for a half hour, etc. HIIT is 10 minutes, but it has you alternate between sprinting full speed for one minute and slowly jogging for another minute, then alternating back and forth until the 10 minutes is up. Although HIIT is much shorter than moderate intensity cardio, you will definitely feel it. Finally, watch your diet. A popular saying among serious bodybuilders goes, "Muscle is built in the kitchen, not in the gym."

To build muscle, your body needs about one gram of protein per pound of bodyweight each day. Good sources are beef, chicken, nuts, tuna, and whey protein powder. Eat frequent, smaller meals rather than three large meals a day. This ensures that your body has enough protein for protein synthesis within your muscles. Eat clean, healthy calories. Avoid trans-fats. (Look for "partially hydrogenated" oils and shortening on ingredient labels). Avoid junk food such as Coke, chips, and white breads. Carbs themselves aren't bad... you just need the right kinds of carbs, like the complex carbohydrates found in oatmeal and whole wheat bread, and fresh veggies and fruit. Avoid starches. Finally, make sure to drink enough fluids, since your muscles are primarily water.

What it means to look good in front of women

Since about 20% to 30% of your attractiveness with girls depends on your looks, when you look more handsome, you'll find that every aspect of your interactions with them will get a boost. Dressing well, working out, and eating sensibly will especially help older guys (30 years old and over). Guys naturally obtain higher status and become more alpha as they age, so if you have a flat stomach as well, it will pay off tremendously.

CHAPTER 6

How to Create an Alpha Male Charisma

Why your Get-up should match your Sex Drive

"Looks are deceptive", and so how you look is important, but definitely not as much as you think. And not in the ways you probably think. Women don't get judged based on how their men look in the same way that we men get judged on how pretty our girlfriends are.

Look at it this way: imagine you're on a vacation, and you meet a chubby girl in a tropical bar who's just as horny as you are. You don't have any other plans for the night, so what would you prefer, having sex with the fat girl, about whom no one will ever find out about, or masturbating alone in your room? Most guys would choose the former. This is assuming that she isn't smelly or hideous — just kind of overweight. "All cats look grey in the dark", as some would say. Besides, who looks at the mantelpiece, when you are stoking the fire?

As long as you meet a certain minimum standard — i.e., you aren't morbidly obese or deformed in a ghastly way — you won't be eliminated because of your ugly mug. Your physical appearance makes up perhaps 20% to 30% of your attractiveness level to women. (Other factors are your level of confidence, how comfortable you are in your skin, how high your status is in society, and how you make women feel in your presence.)

If Johnny Depp — a guy who's a 10 out of 10 in looks (according to my current girlfriend)—were a depressed wimp who slouched all the time and shivered at the thought of speaking to girls he met, he wouldn't have much success at all. So, all things being equal, looking good will certainly add to your attractiveness. In this chapter, you're going to find out the secrets to changing your appearance - as quickly as tonight - that will immediately double or triple your looks.

Physical Fitness

Women used to be able to guess my age before I started exercising six years ago. Sometimes they even guessed older! Then about six months after I started hitting the gym, women I met were surprised at my age — they thought I was much younger. A few months ago, a hot 26 year-old who took me home with her swore I couldn't be older than 28. (I'm 39.) She genuinely didn't believe me when I told her how old I was. I used to be fat and flabby; now I'm slender and muscular. You can't do anything about your genetics. Your fitness level, however, is totally within your control, and it is an important part of what makes you look good to a woman. That's good news for you. Getting in shape will make you look good in so many ways.

Your Skin

One of the easiest (and free) things you can do to improve your sex appeal to women is to get a tan. Obviously, you don't want to go overboard with it, since there's a risk of skin cancer, but sunlight is also necessary for you to get the proper dose of vitamin D, which helps your body produce testosterone. Dark or swarthy complexioned people need not go for a tan - That's just a joke! (Also, lack of sunlight has been linked with depressed moods.) In any event, however, get a nice tan and women will think you're sexy.

Try out a New Hairstyle

If you're like most guys, your hair looks completely atrocious right now. Maybe you've had the same hairstyle for years, or you try to do the same thing with your hair that your friends do with theirs, even though your hair's different. It's high time for you to change. Check out what Hollywood actors and rock stars are doing right now, pick a hairstyle you like, and model yours after it. Of course your hairstyle should be in sync with your age and body structure. Experiment. As I write this guide, "sex hair" (messed up hair that makes you look like you just got out of a woman's bed) is in. Consider going to an expensive hairdresser and giving him or her carte blanche to give you a good style for your head shape. If you really want to look sexy (and you're not homophobic), I recommend going to a gay male hairdresser, since gay guys have an almost supernatural sense of what looks good to women. And honestly, if your hairline has receded to the point where it's highly noticeable, then shave your head. There are a significant percentage of women who consider a shaved head attractive because baldness radiates masculinity and vigor. If you're an older man, then having a shaved head will make you look much younger. Comb-overs fool no one, and few women consider horseshoe-shaped hair to be sexually attractive. But eventually, how you wear your hair really matters to women, BUT PLEASE DON'T LOOK LIKE A GEEK.

Dress Well

For casual, wear shirts that fit, not shirts that look like super baggy. This can be tough, since most clothes you like will not fit. Expect only about 10% of clothes you try on at the store to be suitable. I can't emphasize enough the importance of not wearing baggy, tent-like clothes that are fashionable only in ghetto high schools or among kids. They will not hide your stomach that is bulging out. The best way to obscure your spare tyre is to wear shirts that draw attention to your chest, such as shirts with a horizontal stripe across your man-tits. Wear striped shirts if you are a short person. If you are tall, what you wear, generally, does not matter. Well, again I'm NOT saying that tall guys have an advantage over short guys. Remember, your personality on the whole counts more than looks.

Shaving Tips

Beards or moustaches are generally not in vogue these days, unless you can find a certain look that goes with your features, or if you have some deformity you need to hide. For example, a goatee or beard can work wonders to obscure a weak chin or acne-scarred cheeks. Just as we prefer women to be prim and proper, women too prefer when we're shaved. Shaving your armpits can reduce the amount of bacteria growing under your arms, which reduces foul odors. Also, make sure you don't have unsightly nose hair or hair sticking out of your ears. Many girls find this to be an instant turnoff. You can find an electric nose hair trimmer at your local superstore. Lots of men shave or trim their chests these days, as more women seem to prefer shaved chests to hairy chests. However, that is an individual choice. If you don't care, one way or the other, I suggest testing to see what reactions you get when you shave your chest and wear a shirt that exposes it. If you feel tempted to shave your arms or legs, fight the urge and don't do it. The bottom line is that the vast majority of men who shave these are either (a) professional bodybuilders or (b) gay.

If you are fat, it goes without saying that you should also be hitting the gym (weightlifting and cardio) and eating right so that you can slim down. It also helps with your testosterone levels. Carrying excess body fat (approximately 20% or more above your ideal body weight) can cause your body to have elevated levels of the estrogen hormone. (Ever notice how sometimes really fat guys have "bitch tits"? Now you know why.)

Wear clothes that make you look as close as possible to the ideal male body type, which is tall, with wide shoulders tapering down to a narrow, sleek waist. This is a look that women think is hot! Avoid clothes that make you look different from this ideal body type. For example, fat guys should avoid shirts with horizontal stripes around the waist. If you're tall and thin, try wearing a jacket or unbuttoned long-sleeve shirt over a tight shirt. Horizontal stripes are good; vertical stripes are not. Stay away from anything too common like pinstripes or the ubiquitous polo shirts that fat boys wear. And no, girls will not think you're being original by turning up the collar, since too many guys do that already. Company logos or sports logos on your shirts? That makes it look like you're trying hard to fit in with the pack. That's good if you want to be a generic guy instead of a loser, but it's more attractive to girls if you stand above the pack of guys who are walking billboards.

When dressing casual, you want to give the appearance that you just got dressed after having hot sex with a woman. So don't tuck in your shirt, unless you're wearing a suit. And leave the top two buttons unbuttoned. Avoid cheesy designs or anything that makes it look like you're trying too hard to look cool.

Consider wearing a suit and tie sometimes, especially

when you're in situations where other guys dress like slobs, like in college. Ever notice how women go out of their way to compliment guys wearing suits and ties? A suit and tie are CEO clothes. They communicate status and ambition, and there are no downsides to wearing them. Of course, you should make sure you're alpha on the inside, or you'll come across as a jerk trying hard to make a good impression. When wearing a suit, have a cotton shirt (plain, not with stripes or anything), cuff links, a dark jacket and pants, and black leather, shiny shoes. Wear a nice silk tie, which can even be a bold design. Watch the kind of compliments you get from people. Nothing speaks of authority like a dark suit. Vintage clothes are in, as long as they're not too flamboyant. Jeans are also in. Try getting one pair of expensive jeans. Look for slim fit because you want your legs to look slender. Bagginess conveys femininity because it gives you curves like the female body does.

Shoes are important

I'll talk about shoes first for a good reason: women notice them a lot more than men do. A lot of guys only have a few pairs of shoes in their wardrobe. Have you noticed how many shoes the average woman has? They are highly attuned to what you put on your feet. So make sure your shoes are nice and stylish and even a bit bolder than the plain shoes that the average guy would wear. When you're at a shoe store, definitely ask women about shoes before you buy! You don't want to make an expensive mistake. Just say, "Hey, I need a quick female opinion. Which shoes do you like, this pair or that one?" People respond better to a limited number of choices, so I recommend picking out two pairs at the max that you like the best and then ask for an opinion. Don't worry, if the woman doesn't like either of them, she will probably check out the store's where other shoes are on display and let you know what she likes. (Meanwhile, this has gotten you into an extended conversation with a girl, you sly dog!)

At a bare minimum, you'll need four pairs of shoes:

- Brown casual.
- Black casual.
- Brown dressy.
- Black dressy.

For dressy shoes, I get the kind of shoes that need to be polished. You'll pay for a lot for shoes like that, but they last for years, so they'll be worth the money. When they're shining up, I get lots of compliments. (I've noticed that women really like polished shoes.) For casual, I like to wear short boots. I got a really cool pair of brown boots at a flea market. I get lots of compliments on them from both women and from cool guys. (Whenever cool people compliment you that is a sign that you have achieved "cool" social status.) Boots are also good for shorter guys who want to add a couple of inches to their height. Avoid shoes that make you look like you're trying too hard to fit in, like those branded tennis shoes with the swoosh on them.

Learn Color Coordination

I'm continually amazed at how many guys I see making the most obvious mistakes like wearing brown belts with black shoes, so please pay attention to how the colors of your outfit go together. You need to match all your clothing. You can do these in two ways:

- Through similar colors.
- Through colors that contrast significantly.

Colors tend to affect people's mood and energy level, so think about what you want to convey when you get dressed, and then match up the parts of your outfit accordingly. I'm sure you don't want to stand out as a bizarre sight.

There are two broad categories — warm and cool colors. Warm colors include yellow, orange, and red. Cool colors include purple, blue, and green. If you want to do similar colors, have shades of one color such as light blue jeans and a darker blue shirt. You can also have colors that are closely related — red and purple, for example, both warm colors that are close to each other on the color wheel.

Also dress in colors that are at opposite ends of the color wheel — dark blue jeans with a light brown shirt, for instance.

Neutral colors — white and black — go with almost everything. Also consider wearing colors that are mostly white or black — such as beige, which is white tinted with brown— or grey, which is a combination of black and white. But certainly not beige with grey. The color of your accessories (belt, watch, etc.) should match your shoes as closely as possible. Pants should never contrast all that much with your shoes, although your shirt can.

Another rule for clothes that should be obvious but often is not is that they must be clean. Girls are much more attuned to unlaundered or stained clothes than guys are. How to tell whether clothes need washing:

- On shirts and pants, look for stains. If you see stains, wash the stains out by rinsing the spot under a water faucet and rubbing it with a stain remover. Then toss the article of clothing into the washing machine.

- Socks and underwear should be worn only once and then washed.

- Jeans need to be washed when they get stretched out, even if they're not stained.

- Nothing should smell. If it smells, put it in the laundry. With wrinkle-free fabric so common today, ironing isn't as necessary as it used to be, except in extreme cases. Some things should always be ironed though, such as oxford shirts (the long-sleeved cotton kind that you wear with a suit). When wearing a suit, make sure your shirt is lightly starched, or else you'll look sloppy. Just take your stuff to the dry cleaners and let them do it. Another thing girls appreciate is interesting underwear, since they themselves wear colorful panties. So get something with writing on it or a picture.

How to Cultivate your Unique Style

There are two kinds of guys — those who get laid and those who don't. To get laid, find what demographic of people you fit into, see what the alpha males of that group are wearing, and dress similarly. In particular, just try to be a little bit cooler and unique than most when it comes to your shoes, accessories like your watch or belt, and the way your clothes fit you.

Don't be too cool than everyone else or you'll look out of place and weird. Just be a bit better dressed than the best-dressed guy in the room. Look around, and it'll become obvious to you what looks good on you, and what you should avoid. For example, T-shirts with sports logos, beer bottles, or phrases that you wouldn't say in the polite company are not attractive to girls and typically are worn only by guys who aren't getting laid that night.

Watch the latest hit movies by popular actors for fashion advice. Also check out TV and magazine ads aimed at the 18 to 35 demographic. By that I don't mean clothing ads (since they tend to wear super expensive clothes), but ads for things like cell phones and airlines. The models in those ads are generally dressed subtly cool in a way that appeals to a wide audience. When you're shopping for clothes, get opinions from women in the store. As you come up with your own style that's unique to you, avoid styles that are just too ordinary. I personally like to hit the vintage clothing stores and dress in some of the brighter and tighter early 1980s clothes. That's just me though, as it fits with my personality. So go for something unique and fashionable that is appropriate for who you are, but don't get too wrapped up in how you look. Because, while looking good does help, it's not your looks that get you laid, it's your alpha male behavior and thought patterns.

Women are not just after a good-looking man. They also crave a man with high social status who will give them excitement, passion, and romance. They want a man who will give them a good time and make them feel good. Along with the style issues, it's important also to develop a strong, masculine body. That means working out and having a good diet. Not only will hitting the gym make you look healthier, but you will also feel more energetic and become more attractive to women because you will have so much more confidence.

The most important thing about how you look after all is

said and done, is that it must be consistent and congruent with who you are. Your clothes create perceptions of you in women. So if you can't back up the perceptions you create, then they will be turned off. If your clothes say "excitement" the way a Lamborghini's style does, then women will be disappointed if the motor inside is something conventional like a station wagon or SUV.

CHAPTER 7

How to Avoid these Dating Mistakes

I would like to tell you something from my personal experience. At a very early age, I got my first girlfriend. Even though I was earning, it was just enough to keep body, mind and soul together. The urge to impress my girlfriend led to my spending almost $3,200 on her in one go just to buy her a solitaire and an expensive dinner having the whole month ahead of me and not a penny left in hand. She did sleep with me several times during that span of time, but finally she left me for another guy. I was extremely disheartened after the incident took place, and not to mention the fact that I had to do overtime to earn money.

I have done this mistake, and not just once. There have been many times when I've bought girls dinner, taken them to the movies, bought them jewelery and what not. I was such a spendthrift that I'd routinely take girls out to banquets and buy expensive chocolates on my first date.

A huge amount of money spent, and nothing in return, really disappointed me. All I ever wanted in return was sexual satisfaction, but it was all in vain. The questions that kept perturbing me then were: "Am I asking for a lot? Don't I deserve to get laid after all that I am doing? And I guess it's not just my problem. The case is pretty much the same when it comes to other men. I am sure there are many who are not sexually satisfied after spending a lot. Well, I'll tell you why you are hitting the wrong target. Expensive gifts don't necessarily mean you'll get laid..

The problem with men is that they waste a huge amount of money on women who do not deserve it. This communicates to them that their value is higher than yours, so you need to buy things but do take their consent. But if you believe that your value is high, then you don't need to keep buying her presents even with her consent. On special occasions, you might pick up something small for her at the beginning. She'll appreciate that, but take it easy. Generally, women understand.

CHAPTER 8

How to Get Past her Resistance

How to make her feel at ease with you

Unfortunately, society forces women to believe in logical portions of their minds, rather than in emotional portions that it is sinful to enjoy sex. As women are social creatures more than men are, for reasons of evolutionary psychology, labels such as "slut" or "whore" have a strong negative effect on them. None of these punishments apply to men who have a great amount of sex. Thus, it has become more of a challenge in getting women to do sex than it was back in pre-civilization times when women were bold and free.

So the job of modern man is to get around the social conditioning and draw out the real woman in her. It may sound difficult but trust me, it actually is not. Women are like medicines. They may seem harmful but if you use them for the correct diseases, they can cure your diseases at once. And yes you can do this. I will guide you.

To bring out the real woman that lies hidden inside every girl, one must always keep in mind at a subconscious level, women love sex, and they want it just as much and perhaps even more than men do. And if the social conditions were not enough, a much more powerful force lie within them, that is, their biology. A natural consequence that can result from having an intercourse is having children, and every woman knows it.

Women know that if they conceive when they aren't supposed to people will point fingers. They're dead scared of the social condemnation. They don't mind giving you a nice bulge if the place and situation are right. They love romance, but the atmosphere must be in sync as well. Thus, they can't be free with their sexuality without being labeled a whore. So it is essential for you as a sexual man while progressing with women towards sex, to prevent them from facing it like a whore.

Your main aim is to win a relationship with a woman long-term, not to just have a temporary Such temporary pleasure can be ascertained from a brothel, with a literal whore. You are looking for the woman of your dream and life, and once you win her, with much deliberation of course, you must know how to keep her long.

Since it is evident that women like sex, it's okay to have sex as one's agenda while mixing (or interacting) with women. It is, in fact, a great idea if handled correctly (or carefully). What is to be avoided, however, is verbalizing your motives. You should not say anything about sex, that you want to have it, to the woman you are with.

Once you reveal your desire of having sex to a woman, by saying something about it, you attack the logical portion of her mind, which leads her societal conditioning to kick in, and she starts feeling that the guy she is with, is tacky, gross and animal-like, and she is not in safe hands.

Once again, I repeat, verbalizing might just work with certain women of the lower status and may work with the one you've already got as your chick. A respectable woman will only give herself into your hands so to speak, once she is assured of your long-term commitment. So just watch what you say and certainly, watch what you do.

Avoid being outspoken or direct about sex, but do keep in the back of your mind how much women love sex, and work on projecting your desire of sex without saying anything about it. Use your Body language instead of your mouth.

Be Discreet

There is a proper method which human being's take into consideration while mating. It's just like a dance, and it lasts only for a few hours. Only if this method is correctly followed, it will lead to sex and not otherwise. However, men do have a tendency of being outspoken and restless. They directly want to know their current status in the relationship and how the woman feel with him. This is a grave mistake.

One should never speak anything about where one stands in a relationship. Never let the girl know about your intentions. You will be very silly if you do that as this will lead to her thinking that you are an opportunist, and will kill the emotions. And I had already said that this is not good as emotions are a must for woman to have in order to be uninhibited and ready for sex.

Her thoughts about Sex

Don't believe when they speak about the kind of men they prefer, instead keep a watch on their behavior and observe the type of man they actually choose. If women were honest, they would have said that the kind of man they like is a sexual man who creates opportunities for intercourse and who successfully conquers their barriers. However, some women are outspoken and may tell you straight that they just love sex, but are perhaps choosy about their men. But most will not even utter this as they are terrified of someone calling them sluts, whores or prostitutes.

I do not deny the fact that women like relationships, but that is not something they need a man for. After all, they have very intimate relationships with their female friends. All that a woman wants a man for is to provide her with good sex, not forgetting the security part as well. And this is because women assume that they have a passive role when it comes to sex.

Don't force her to take the initiative. Women live in fear of the slut label. How can you expect her to initiate sex? It is, in fact, impossible on her part and very daft on your part to expect that to happen. To get in bed, you have to create situations where the woman feels that she can sleep with you without fearing about the consequences. You have to be very tactful, if you want to make the move toward asking her to go to bed with you. You need to be humorous, smart and always giving her reassurance of your love. She will make love to you, not if you keep bringing up the subject of sex to her directly. Remember, she is shy when it comes to making the first moves, but once she sleeps with you, you literally then have her on your toast.

If you are successful in making her believe that you are a gentle man, and if she really hit it off with you, she'll start believing that, even if she does have sex on her first date, you were an exception, and she has no regrets. Always remember one thing, a good time for a woman is a good sign for a man. And once you take the lead the effort will be worthwhile.

CHAPTER 9

How to Charm her with Words

When to Compliment her tactfully

You must not observe reality and then work in accordance with it. Instead, you must work out your own reality, which means you must act in a very natural way- the way things normally work out and are meant to work out. Don't try and re-invent the wheel.

For those people looking up to you, don't necessarily mean that it is enough for them to like you. If you come across as too high in status than theirs, they will get nervous and start thinking that the two of you do not share a good chemistry together, as they just don't feel comfortable and very good about themselves when they are around you. This is because they believe you to be much better than themselves.

This is a problem faced by lot of people who are believed to be "cool". They are actually a class apart, and thus, others get jittery about them. As a result, a lot of these cool people actually have trouble maintaining relationships (both sexual relationships and friendships). So what you should do is balance your coolness by making them feel comfortable and enabling the people you interact with to feel good about themselves when you are around.

And how will you do that? You do it by giving out genuine compliments. One way of doing this is making a flattering observation and then quickly asking a question after that in a querying manner, as if you are trying to be sure as to whether the woman is qualified to be with you or not. If you make her feel that you are a good catch, she will feel great when she impresses you.

Examples –

You: "You have an amazing energy about you. What do you do for fun?"
Her: "Blah blah"

You (thinking about it for a second): "Hey, that does sound like fun. I'd love to hear more about it."
You: You seem really cool. What do you study at school?"
Her: "Blah blah."
You: "Interesting! I have a friend who studied blah blah."

When you give a genuine compliment, quickly follow it with a question relating to the topic. This stops the woman from denying the compliment, and it also makes her prove herself to you. As long as you make her feel qualified to be with you, she will believe everything you say and do anything for you. An alpha male doesn't need an approval in return of an approval. He only gives

106

approval. So you shouldn't wait for her to thank you for the compliment you have given her.

You also need to do this because women generally deny compliments, because many of them view themselves in a lesser light. And they may think you are falsely flattering them, which is the last thing they should do. So don't give her the opportunity to deny your appreciation.

I personally follow my compliment with a question so as to make her feel that even though I found something about her which I like, my approval can still be taken away if I don't like her answer. This makes her want to impress me all the more and when she finds out that she has actually impressed me with her answers, she is overjoyed.

Now, here's something you need to watch: it's important that you don't give out fake compliments because then you're trying actually too hard for approval. Besides, it's tough to give a fake compliment and have it sound sincere, and you definitely don't want her to get suspicious. 'Beta's suck up to women, alpha don't have to. Another strategy I like, particularly with a new woman, is to quickly change the subject after complimenting her. "You seem really cool. Hey, you know what? On my drive over here, I saw . . .." That keeps me in control of the conversation's direction, plus prevents her from having the chance to deny my compliment. Another reason I like to sprinkle compliments in my interactions with people is that it keeps me externally focused. Because I'm thinking about them, I'm not burdened with worrying and over-analyzing my every move.

CHAPTER 10

How to Show that You are the Man for Her

Why be Assertive but never Aggressive

What do you think is the one thing that makes women most attracted to the alpha man? It's the impression that you're a dominant man. And no, you don't have to grunt, scratch, and slap a woman around like a cave man to convey dominance. You convey your dominant male status simply by acting the way dominant men do, by being careful about the non-verbal cues you send out, thereby creating the impression within a woman that you are 'alpha'. This technique is known as the association principle. By doing this, you are associating yourself with desirable masculine traits within the minds of women, while dissociating yourself from undesirable "nice guy" traits.

One thing you never do and that is showing a woman how desperate you are. She will just think you are a weakling and will take you for granted.

This is how magicians operate. On stage, the magician carefully controls the audience's impression of him. By diverting the audience's attention towards things that they associate with magic — like his waving wand and saying magical spells, he prevents the audience from noticing the thing that would make him look non-magical: the fact that he's actually using his hand to do the trick!

Similarly, you can use impression management to control what the woman thinks of you. You are the subject. What you need to do is to try and take her off yourself and allow her to concentrate on something else. You need not talk about yourself all the time. Be a bit cocky and arrogant, but don't overdo it.

In fact, never overdo anything, good or bad. Learn to

strike a balance. Life is all about striking a balance. And you too can start making changes from today itself by adopting the behavior of an alpha male. So what's dominance? It's power, which comes from assertiveness. As you go through your process of self-improvement, eventually you will imbibe the concepts of this book and become an alpha male.

Your eyes are the foremost nonverbal cue which indicates that you're an alpha male. A dominant man is not afraid to gaze directly at people. It is very important to make eye contact with people. It indicates your self-confidence. It also shows that you are not shy and slimy. By averting your gaze, you communicate submissiveness. When you look down, you communicate self-consciousness, shame, guilt, and a sense of low status.

When it is you who is talking, there is no limit as to how much eye contact you can make. Studies have shown that the more eye contact the person doing the talking makes, the more dominant the listener perceives that person to be and is more attentive while listening. However, when you're the one doing the listening, the opposite is true: the less you look at the other person while they're talking, the more dominant you become. (Ever wonder why adults tell children, "Look at me when I'm talking to you?" It's a way of reinforcing the adult's dominance over the child.) Of course, you don't want to go overboard and have the woman think you're staring her down.

If you're thought to be as too dominant, then your likability starts to suffer. So give your eyes a break every now and then. Another indicator of your dominance is your voice. Dominant people control the conversation. They also speak in a cutting voice and aren't afraid to intervene when the other person is speaking. Studies have shown that using a soft, quiet voice can give off the impression that you are neither assertive nor confident.

When you speak, try to let your words flow and don't be afraid to speak your mind. People who hesitate and start mumbling are perceived as less powerful than those who do not. Watch your mannerisms and behaviors.

Try to avoid the following nonverbal indicators of beta status:

- Using "ah" and "um," partial sentences, and partial words. Studies have shown that people consider others who talk like this to lack confidence and not be too bright. It's a sign of nervousness. The reason we say "um" is because we're afraid we're going to be interrupted by the other person. Instead, don't be afraid to pause for effect. Pausing before important points will make you seem more competent and people will remember what you say.

- Speaking too fast. This gives off the impression

that you feel anxious and have low self-confidence. A normal, comfortable speaking rate varies within a moderate range from 125 to 150 words per minute. First marshal your thoughts, and then speak and speak confidently to the person.

- Speaking with a monotonous voice, also known as mumbling. People with a narrow pitch range are viewed as unassertive, uninteresting, and lacking in confidence. So vary your pitch and you will be perceived as outgoing and alpha.

- Pausing too long before responding to a question. This indicates that you're thinking too hard for your answer, which makes you seem indecisive, one lacking a good deal of confidence. It also looks like you're trying too hard to win the other person's approval. Just talk as you normally would, right?

- Twitching your fingers or hands. When you're across the table from someone there's a natural inclination to play with sugar packets or straw wrappers with your fingers. Don't. And don't drum your fingers on the table — women hate that.

- Touching your face when you talk. This indicates that you're thinking too hard, you're indecisive, or that you feel shy. To convey confidence, hold your hands together in a steeple shape in front of your chest or face. (A lot of professors do this when they are lecturing.) Another posture that will help you when you need a huge display of confidence is holding your hands at your hips. Cops do this when they need to establish authority over criminal suspects. Well, you don't want to give the cop impression to her, but you should assert yourself more than anything else, in a tactful manner of course.

- Looking down. The alpha man holds his head high. It shows zest. Looking down at the floor telegraphs "loser." Keep your chin up. Expose your neck — don't worry, nobody's going to choke you! Look at the person you're talking to; remember what I said about using your eyes.

- Nervous facial gestures such as lip licking, pursing your lips, twitching your nose, and biting your lips. An alpha male has a relaxed face and mouth because he fears no one.

- Excessive smiling. Studies of primates have shown that beta males will smile as a way to signal their harmlessness to stronger males. Beta humans smile to show they're not a threat. The alpha male, however, only smiles when there is something to smile about. And yes — he can be a threat.

- Walking fast as part of your normal walk. Instead,

walk a little slower than normal, almost as if you're swaggering. You're Alpha — no one's chasing you and you're not rushing to please anyone else. If you're not in a hurry to get somewhere, walk like you're relaxed and confident. Think: "I am the man. I can make any woman happy."

- Walking only with your legs. Don't be afraid to move your torso and arms. Try this: walk as if you'd just had a massive success and felt on top of the world. Watch what you do with your body. You may find yourself moving your arms along with your shoulders and having a slight bounce in your step. Now, do that all the time.

- Slouching. You don't have to stand uncomfortably ramrod straight, but you should have your shoulders back. Watch Brad Pitt in any of his movies for examples of how to comfortably hold your back straight. (I keep bringing Brad Pitt up because he provides an excellent example of what good body language looks like. Also watch George Clooney. For fans of older movies, check out Sean Connery in From Russia With Love and Rock Hudson in Pillow Talk.)

- Blinking a lot. Instead blink your eyes slowly. Don't close your eyes in discomfort. Just let your eyelids relax. In fact, let them droop a bit. Don't be bug-eyed.

- Shifting your eyes back and forth when you speak. That's very beta. When you're in a conversation and you're doing the talking, gaze at the other person's face. Nonverbally, this communicates that that you say is important and worth listening to.

- Holding too much eye contact when the other person speaks. Ignore the dating advice books that tell you to hold non-stop eye contact. Non-stop eye contact makes you look needy, socially retarded, and, frankly, like a weirdo. Instead let your eyes blur and then gaze at her eyes. Look through her rather than at her. From extensive testing, I've found that gazing at a woman about two-thirds of the time is optimal. By the way, only hold the gaze when she's telling you something genuinely interesting. Otherwise, focus on other stuff like her breasts, her hair, things going on around you, etc.

- Being afraid to touch a woman, and thus being 'non-touching' beta. Be confident about it when you touch women--any nervousness at all can be fatal to your relations with her. Be alpha and physically move her when you need to. Hold her hand to lead her around, etc. Be gentle — if you use excessive pressure, you reveal your insecurity. (Since you're alpha, of course she will follow you, so there's no need to be anything other than playful and tender.) It's natural to touch others, as when you're emphasizing a point. So let the love flow!

- Turning your head fast when someone wants your attention. Instead use the movements that you would when you're at home — slow and relaxed. You're not at anyone's beck and call. You're alpha, remember this basic fact always. Nobody is going to tell you that. You need to understand that YOU ARE AN ALPHA MALE, RIGHT?

- Circumlocution- Alphas keep it short and to the point. If you're tempted to use long sentences, break them up. Don't feel bad if you inevitably slip up and use some of these nonverbal cues from time to time. No one's perfect, so don't beat yourself up about it, especially when you're talking with a woman. Let it go and keep the conversation moving. When you think about such things too much while talking, you start to doubt yourself, and when that happens, you feel insecure and anxious and become hesitant. Instead just work on remaining nonchalant, yet sincere and true at all times. It's enough to simply be aware of how you communicate non-verbally to everyone you do, because being aware means you will start to avoid negative communications much more.

What are the specific Beta Male Behaviors to Avoid

Mentally speaking, we as humans are more prone to think negatively about other people and various things around us. Very seldom will you hear people speaking in positive light about others. Sometimes, you might have experienced talking to someone and then suddenly, he or she says something out of the way that sort of puts you totally off, and your opinion about that one changes, without hesitation. Then whatever previous talk you might have been enjoying, just pales into insignificance. You now perhaps consider him or her some biological freak, and that too based on that one thing he or she might have said, thoughtlessly.

Hence, make a conscientious effort to stop thinking in a negative manner about anybody, without having proper and concrete evidence; or else people, especially other men will rate you very low, and you will fall below your own status, as a male. You've got to think like a mature individual in order to win over the woman of your choice. It takes effort, and it won't happen in a day. You've got to work hard on this trait, if you have this streak in you. Just go through a few suggestions, given here in order to strengthen your ties with women.

The beta characteristics to avoid are:

- Sometimes your sentences, laced with question tags, "is it so ?" or "that's correct.", must be used appropriately because she can easily detect certain strains of you passionately desiring approval from her. You must never make her feel that you are dying for her to say, "yes", to your relationship with her. Just have very casual and normal conversations.

- If you are by nature a domineering person, you can do so in a polite and unassuming manner. The woman should never get the impression that you are bossing her around. Have a stronger mind of your own. Don't give in to their whims and fancies all the time, but you must also try and be more understanding, caring and above all, loving in your attitude toward them. Even in the forces, the higher rank officers are generally quite polite when it comes to getting work done by their subordinates. Sometimes, you may need to give in but this does not lower your male status in any way. Don't feel that way, if ever you are in such a situation.

- Being violent or throwing your male weight around with either men or women, does not speak well of you. It bespeaks a very low status as a male. I know many males who resort to physical force, especially with their partners when the situation seems to go out of control. You needn't worry about this. A woman's weapon is her tongue and a man's his hands. So do not even think of resorting to such a method of resolving your issues with your woman. The wisest thing to do when such a serious situation arises is to walk out of the scene, and only return when matters have cooled down-perhaps after a couple of hours. But violence will never solve your problems. It will only compound them. Don't ever think that she will be enthralled by your strong arms or good built.

- You have got to learn to be a good listener. Women love those men who have the patience to listen to all their stories, even if some of them are disinteresting or stupid. You must develop this habit of listening to her, even if the topic of conversation is not your cup of tea. If you closely observe an alpha male, like the CEO of a big company or a political leader, you will notice that they only love to talk about themselves. When an alpha male is getting cheesed off with a conversation, he simply switches off by turning his head away and displays unconcern. You must let people, especially women, earn your attention.

- Never feel that you know it all. Well, you might definitely know a great deal, but avoid showing off your intelligence. You will not be appreciated for it. You will only earn the disrespect of those listening to you. There are times when you need to listen to what others have to say, especially if you do not have any idea about the subject under discussion. The biggest leaders and highly intelligent ones are generally and truly exceptionally good listeners. Big Directors and CEO'S of top companies are some people who try to improve their knowledge by listening closely to other experts in other fields. Don't you consider this a very vital point?

- Having a roving eye is again something you need to avoid. Looking at every sexy bomb in town is not going to add bonuses to your male status. As one of my close buddies would say, "If it moves; nail it." A guy who is getting massively laid sees no point in trying to gain cheap popularity by checking out other babes in his neighborhood. So try and let it work the other way around with you. Let the women check you out for a change, and be impressed with your looks or attitude. Give them a chance to try and win your approval. Just do it and see if it works. You'll be surprised to get fantastic results.

The Alpha Male naturally feels he is a born leader and displays this attitude, wherever he goes. He simply ignores what others say and think nothing of them, and what they have to say. He just goes ahead and does what he feels and thinks best. This is definitely a very self-centered attitude, but despite this attitude of his, he gains a following. This is probably because he is an interesting person to talk to, and can keep you enthralled with his selection of topics, and moreover, when others see his followers, they too get attracted.

Why are his topics of conversation so interesting? It is because he selects those subjects that he finds fascinating and that those of his followers find interesting as well.

What's the easiest way to have something to discuss about? It's not difficult at all. You just need to be exciting and well-balanced, and you can openly display your attraction toward women. You need to keep yourself busy all the time with your own life and day-to-day activities, so that your mind is always thinking. Do not remain idle by simply sitting and watching television. Go out to the club and involve yourself in a game of snooker, perhaps. You may chill out with some of your close pals if you want. However, don't sit at home doing nothing. Basically, when your hands are full, you will find many interesting topics to discuss. When talking to women, you be in control of the topics and get their attention.

As soon as you start working on your attitude you will quickly start developing the mindset of an alpha male. What I have noticed is that all alpha males know that they will have a following, and they do not act bossy. They are confident about themselves. Try to avoid being the bossy male and just concentrate on your own work because most people do not like to be shoved around the place. If you just go about your own business, you will get followers.

You must not observe reality and then work in accordance with it. Instead, you must work out your own reality, which means you must act in a very natural way-the way things normally work out and are meant to work out. Don't try and re-invent the wheel, as it were.

Just behave normal. Act as though 'pussy' doesn't matter to you, and it is actually not a big deal for men who are getting laid all the time. You may not be that quintessential, sexy guy, but you may still want to style yourself after such men. You don't have to conceal your sex drive, the way some do, but just act naturally. Behave like a normal male, and your rating will automatically go up. Don't lose sleep over what women might think of you, because your thinking is far more important than the way they think of you. You will also find, rather ironically, that they will render more respect to you than you originally thought.

A great number of men get the wrong notion that women think wrongly of them, and they just can't get over it. "When she smacks her lips and acts smutty, does it mean that she's got the hots for me?" [When a woman smacks her lips or rubs a glass sensually, that is indeed an attraction signal.] You must not worry. Just keep in mind that she is feeling horny and wants you in bed with her to hump her badly. All you have to do is take it easy, relax and behave as though you have not got the green signal from her until she catches your collar and starts making those passionate moves. If she does not make the right moves, it will be equivalent to her loss. You've got nothing to lose. You may give her some leads in order for her to continue in a horny manner.

Don't be a 'wuss'. Be confident and positive in your outlook. Have you noticed how the best athletes like Carl Lewis, Michael Jordan and Roger Federer know that they will make it? They never chicken out of a situation. They have tremendous confidence in themselves. Success stems from confidence.

You have to show an irresistible attitude toward women if you desire them badly. Work against your natural inclinations and you will emerge a winner. Trust me on this. You must be strong and un-shakeable. All the same, be yourself, full of beans. You need to be a bit on the naughty side too and think you are an exciting person whom women will want. Always be true to yourself and don't be dishonest. If you do not wish to do something then don't go ahead with it.

What am I trying to say? Well, if you feel like helping a needy child, then do it. If you think a blind man requires your help to cross the street, then help him if you want, but just do what pleases you, right? Remember that you're the kind of sweet, naughty devil that women are looking out for. They don't want a stupid, saucy, unattractive man. They want the best and they have some idea as to who to choose.

Finally, you will be a true alpha male if you are honest, genuine and true to yourself.

CHAPTER 11

Conclusion

As you take control of your thoughts and attitude and reach out for your dream babes in life, you will realize that you're becoming genuinely happy in a way that you've never felt before. With women, you'll be so successful and attractive that you will never have to pretend to be someone else to get sex.

I'll sum up by repeating a truly amazing psychological technique I've talked about throughout this guide... proven through decades of complete practical research on my part. The technique is so simple... yet greatly effective and nearly impossible for most guys to figure out on their own, because they engage themselves in too much self-analysis.

The technique is simply this:

1. Don't self-analyze at all when you're with a woman. Just accept things the way they come, naturally.

2. Maintain the dominant frame in all your dealings.

3. Control your own perceptions of reality.

Just do the above three things, and you will achieve the dreams that used to be your wildest fantasies. In fact, you'll literally be able to make any woman dripping wet for you... with just your mind! Truly be yourself. Share yourself and get to know women. Do what you want with them... be romantic, have sex, whatever.

Remember: You're in this life to enjoy yourself and be happy. Not tomorrow, but today. Finally, keep this in mind. With this guide, you've learnt everything you need to know to become an alpha male. And please don't be judgmental, because all women are different.

Good luck!

Made in the USA
Middletown, DE
01 November 2022